GROSS and Frightening ANIMAL FACTS

BIZARRE ANiMaLS

Stella Tarakson

MASON CREST

THAT'S BIZARRE!

Mason Crest
450 Parkway Drive, Suite D
Broomall, Pennsylvania 19008
(866) MCP-BOOK (toll free)

First printing
9 8 7 6 5 4 3 2 1

ISBN (hardback) 978-1-4222-3924-7
ISBN (series) 978-1-4222-3923-0
ISBN (ebook) 978-1-4222-7861-1

Cataloging-in-Publication Data on file with the Library of Congress

Bizarre Animals
Text copyright © 2015 Pascal Press Written by Stella Tarakson

First published 2015 by Pascal Press PO Box 250, Glebe, NSW 2037 Australia

Publisher: Lynn Dickinson Principal Photographer: Steve Parish © Nature-Connect Pty Ltd
Additional Photography: See p. 48 Researcher: Clare Thomson, Wild Card Media Editor: Vanessa Barker

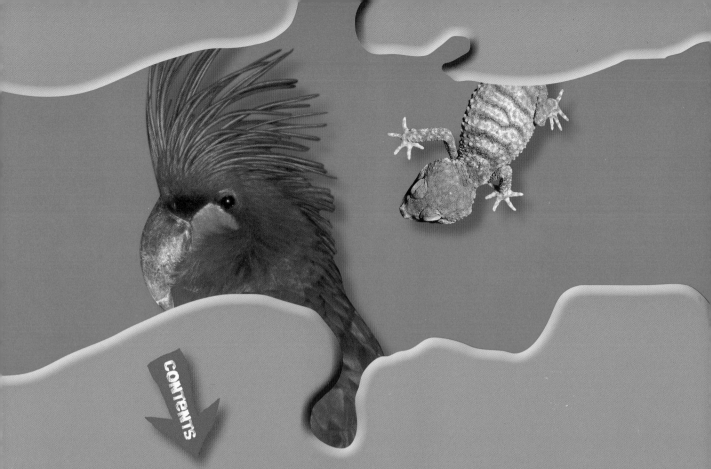

THAT'S BIZARRE!

CHAPTER 1

THAT'S MONSTROUS!

There's big, there's huge, and then there's monstrous! Snakes and lizards and bugs may be fine when they're small, but when they start to tower over you — that's when things get bizarre!

DOES MY BOTTOM LOOK BIG IN THIS?

Man-sized meal

So maybe your dad eats a lot, but even he can't match a blue whale! These massive beasts eat crustaceans called krill. Because krill are so small (about 7 inches [7.5 centimeters]), a whale needs to eat 7,937 pounds (3.6 tonnes) of krill a day just to feel full!

GIMME WHAT'S LEFT ON YOUR PLATE!

NICE DAY FOR A DIP

Would you like to go for a swim — inside a whale? The blue whale is so gigantic its heart is the size of a small car. You could even swim through its blood vessels! A fully grown blue whale is the largest mammal that's ever lived and can weigh as much as 33 elephants.

A heart as big as a car!
(a small car)

SINGIN' THE BLUES
The blue whale is bigger than the biggest dinosaur. Now that's something to sing about!

You know the old song, "Never smile at a crocodile…" Well, here's one you wouldn't want to get friendly with! The Australian estuarine crocodile is the largest living reptile on Earth. The average adult male is 16 feet (5 meters) long and weighs a whopping 1,012 pounds (450 kilograms) — and it wouldn't mind snapping you up for dinner!

CROCO-DIAL TRIPLE ZERO

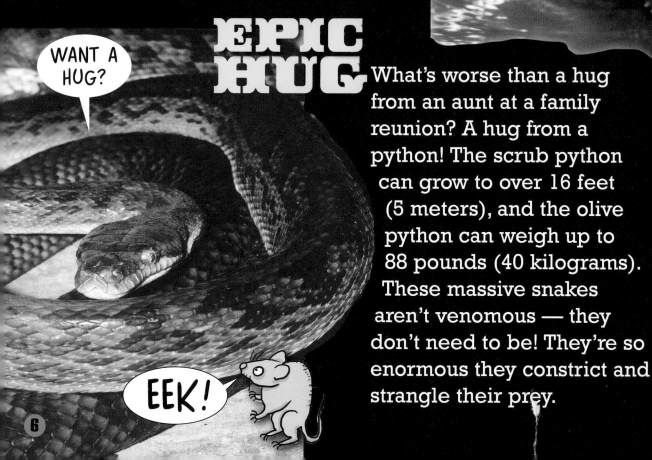

EPIC HUG

WANT A HUG?

What's worse than a hug from an aunt at a family reunion? A hug from a python! The scrub python can grow to over 16 feet (5 meters), and the olive python can weigh up to 88 pounds (40 kilograms). These massive snakes aren't venomous — they don't need to be! They're so enormous they constrict and strangle their prey.

EEK!

RING! RING!

WHAT DID I SWALLOW?

Did you know that the world's biggest lizard can kill humans? The Komodo dragon weighs over 300 pounds (136 kilograms) and measures up to 10 feet (3 meters). But don't worry, this overgrown relative of the goanna is only found on a few Indonesian islands! Phew!

ENTER THE DRAG

I'M SUPPOSED TO BE EATING YOU!

CAUGHT IN THE WEB

The golden orb spider may look scary, but its venomous bite is nonlethal to humans. The spider's golden-colored web is so strong it can catch even birds and bats! Bat bacon for breakfast, anyone?

SIP, SUCK, SLURP!

A numbat has terrible table manners, not to mention strange taste in food! It uses its bizarrely long tongue to suck up fat, juicy termites. It doesn't even stop to chew. With a tongue half the length of its body, saying "Aaaah" is not so easy!

I DON'T EVEN NEED A STRAW!

DON'T BUG ME

The giant burrowing cockroach makes a great pet — if you don't want something cuddly! Weighing 1 ounce (30 grams), it's the world's biggest cockroach. It's even bigger than a mouse! The cockroach's long life span also means you'll have your six-legged sidekick for a good 10 years.

BIG MOMMA

Imagine giving birth to 3,000 babies every day! That's just what the termite queen does. This giant, fat white blob produces thousands of babies deep inside the termite mound, where she lives for 20–50 years. Lucky this monstrous mother has thousands of smaller termites to do the housework for her!

GENTLE GIANT

Whale sharks may be sharks by name but not by nature. Growing up to 66 feet (20 meters) in length, this fish looks formidable! Lucky for us, its taste is like the blue whale's — it prefers krill to a meatier menu!

I SAID KRILL, NOT KILL!

THE NOSE HAS IT

A male elephant seal can weigh up to 8,157 pounds — that's 3.7 tonnes (3,700 kilograms)! With a length of up to 16 feet (5 meters), that makes it bigger and longer than most cars. It is also known for its trunk-like snout.

ARE YOU CALLING ME AN ELEPHANT?

FACT OR FICTION?

Shiver me timbers! Sea legends describe a massive sea monster called the Kraken, which would attack ships with its long tentacles. Sailors thought it was just a story — until scientists discovered a giant squid as long as a bus living deep in the ocean. That's some colossal calamari!

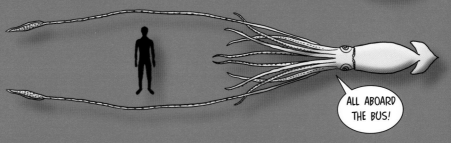

ALL ABOARD THE BUS!

43 feet (13 meters)

CHAPTER 2

BRAINS!

When it comes to being clever, you need a big brain — right? Wrong! A larger brain doesn't always mean a smarter animal. Big bodies need big brains just to keep them going. It's the size of your brain compared to your body that counts in the smarts stakes.

OH YEAH!

BODY SIZE vs BRAIN SIZE

NOT BAD!

MARSUPIALS IN ORDER OF BRAININESS
(BRAIN SIZE TO BODY SIZE)

STRIPED POSSUM	320
LONG-TAILED PYGMY POSSUM	266
BENNETT'S TREE-KANGAROO	246
KANGAROOS & WALLABIES	193
BRUSHTAIL POSSUMS	192
RINGTAIL POSSUMS	139

WHICH WAY DID HE GO?

NOT FAIR!

SMARTY PANTS

While humans don't have the biggest brains in the world, we have good-sized brains compared to our bodies. We've used our intelligence to make many incredible things — just look around you! However, other animals use their brains in ways we can't. Bees communicate by dancing, and birds use magnetic fields to navigate. And don't forget — we smart humans sometimes still do very dumb things!

BRAIN FOOD

Are dolphins smarter than people? Their brains are bigger than ours — 3.5 pounds (1.6 kilograms) compared to 2.9 pounds (1.3 kilograms). Bottlenose dolphins are so smart that they teach their young to put sponges on their noses to help them find food in rough places, like rocky reefs. Bet your parents never taught you that!

WHO DROPPED THE SPONGE?

NO GENIUS

Koalas have teensy-weensy brains. Their brains weigh 0.6 ounces (17 grams), which is about the size of a cherry tomato. Don't ask them to do long division!

1 + 2 = TREE

EX-CELL-ENT

The more brain cells an animal has, the more complex its brain. Humans have around 100,000,000,000 brain cells! In comparison, a tiny cockroach has around 1,000,000 brain cells, while a fruit fly has only 250,000. That's something we should cell-ebrate!

USE YOUR BRAINS!

Your brain isn't just for homework. No matter what your teacher says, you're using your brain all the time—when you smell, when you breathe, when you run ... even when you sleep! Like all animals, we use our brains without even knowing it!

HAVE YOU DONE YOUR HOMEWORK?

YUMMY

Brain surgeons say the human brain has the same soft and squishy texture as tofu. Yummy! Fancy vegetarian stir-fry for dinner tonight?

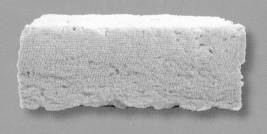

BRAIN BLENDER

If you put a human adult's brain in a blender, you'd make around 8 cups (2 liters) of gooey brain smoothie. That's one barf-ilicious beverage!

FRESH BRAINS DRINK
CARBONATED FLAVOR SOFT DRINK

BRAIN WAVES

Breaking news — 6.5-foot (2-meter)- wide brain found on ocean floor! Oops, sorry, false alarm— it's just a brain coral, a giant coral that looks like ... yep, you guessed it!

CROW IN THE KNOW

Bird-brained? Not quite! Crows are very smart creatures. They can even use specially designed vending machines. Crows can pick up coins, insert them into a machine, then eat a peanut that comes out. But are they smart enough to know they're being ripped off?

I'M WORKING FOR PEANUTS.

SERVE YOURSELF 15¢

LIFT FOR MERCHANDISE

LOCKATOO

Scientists found that cockatoos can solve a complicated puzzle with five locks in order to get to food. Lock and load!

CHATTERING CHICKENS

Chickens have tiny, nut-sized brains, but they're still able to "talk" to each other. Before you go comparing this to your sister and her friends, read on. Scientists have found that chickens use 24 different sounds to communicate! This includes a quiet, high-pitched "eeeee" sound when they see a threat from above, like a hungry bird of prey.

WHAT DID YOU SAY ABOUT DRUMMERS?

A SMART DRUMMER?

Male palm cockatoos have a hidden musical talent! It's not just their wild punk hairdos. They break small sticks off trees and use them to drum on hollow tree trunks, marking their territory. Other cockatoos are known to throw stones and twigs to defend themselves from birds of prey. Rock and roll!

CHAPTER 3

EYEBALLS!

Think all eyes are the same? Think again! Humans and other mammals have camera-style eyes with a single lens. Smaller creatures — such as insects, spiders and crabs — have compound eyes with lots of little lenses. If we had compound eyes, they'd have to be humongous for us to see well. Imagine the size of your sunglasses!

LOTSA LENSES

While a human has just 2 lenses — one on each eye — the Cairns birdwing butterfly has an impressive 10,000 lenses!

PINHOLE PEEPHOLE

Have you ever seen an old-fashioned pinhole camera? Be glad you don't have eyes like that! The nautilus does. It's a primitive animal known as a "living fossil" that lives deep in the ocean. They don't have lenses like other animals but instead have a small pinhole-type eye that only lets them see basic images.

THE EYES HAVE IT

Eyes have evolved over 500 million years — from the pinhole eyes of the nautilus to our current complex eyes. But we can't see well in the dark, and there are some types of light (like UV) that we can't see at all. Maybe our sight is still not eye-deal!

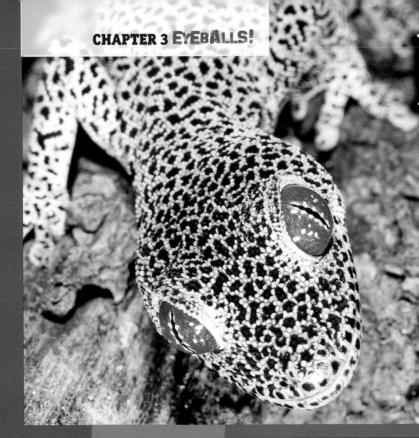

Lickety Spit

Wouldn't it be creepy to have no eyelids? Geckos don't! Instead, they have a clear covering on their eyes. They use their tongues to lick them clean — a bit like windshield wipers!

A SIGHT FOR SORE EYES

Don't challenge a snake to a staring contest — it'll never lose. Snakes don't blink because they have no eyelids! Instead, their eyes are covered with something like a self-repairing contact lens. Scientists are looking at copying this for humans — it could give us super vision!

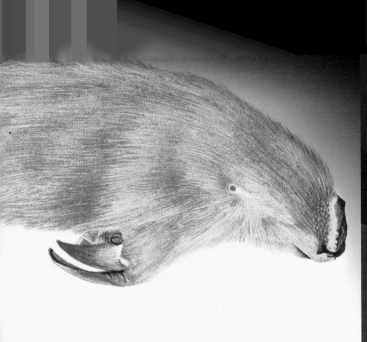

BLIND DATE

Having hollow, sightless eyeballs might seem pointless to us, but they're perfect for the marsupial mole! They don't need to see since they spend most of their time burrowing underground in the dark.

HARD TO SWALLOW

Next time you have trouble swallowing your veggies, just be glad you're not a frog! Frogs can't chew. Instead, their eyes sink into their skulls to help push the food down. No wonder they croak!

CHAPTER 4

BODY BITS

Weird animals have all kinds of strange body parts: tusks and tails and wings and hooves. Some have normal-looking bits with crazy functions that you couldn't even imagine! Super-long tongues? Knobbly tails? That's just the beginning!

Knock Knock

Who's there? The knob-tailed gecko! These creatures have strange knobs on the end of their tails — but don't confuse them with doorknobs, or you might get bitten! Scientists think these geckos vibrate the knobs to distract predators.

NAILED IT!

Nailtail wallabies have a hidden secret. They have a small spur, or nail, on the end of their tails! No one really knows why. Maybe these wallabies use the spur for fighting or for making fast turns while running by jabbing it into the ground. Maybe they like popping bubble wrap. We just don't know!

SPEC-TUSK-ULAR!

TUSK TUSK!

What kinds of animals have tusks? Elephants. Walruses. Warthogs. Frogs. Frogs?! Yep, you heard right. Just like the others, male tusked frogs use their curved tusks as weapons to fight each other. On guard!

GROUND-BOUND BIRDY

Not all birds can fly. That applies to the emu, which is Australia's largest bird. They do have wings, but they're just clumps of feathers and useless when it comes to flying. That's a good thing because big birds mean big poos! You wouldn't want an emu flying overhead and dropping a big one on you!

FINGER FOOD

Striped possums love munching on fat, juicy beetle larvae. They have a special long fourth finger that is perfect for hooking them out of tree trunks — like the way little brothers hook out balls of snot! Om nom nom!

SNOT GOOD...

Fancy DRESS

The frill-neck lizard sure knows how to make an entrance. He has a big, bright orange collar made of scaly skin that unfolds when he opens his mouth. This helps him scare away predators, attract mates and set fashion trends!

SNAKES WITH **LEGS?**

Is it a lizard? Is it a snake? Sometimes it's hard to tell! Some lizards only have back legs to paddle through the sand. Others spend all their time burrowing underground and have no legs at all. They'd only get in the way!

TONGUE TWISTER

"Tongues with tentacles" sounds like the title of a horror movie! But these animals are real — and maybe even in your backyard! Rainbow lorikeets feed on pollen and nectar. Their tongues have tiny tentacles to help them out, just like sea anemones.

PLASTIC FANTASTIC

This may look like a plastic bag floating past, but it's actually a jellyfish! The Venus comb girdle is like a long see-through ribbon. It can grow to almost 5 feet (1.5 meters) long but is only about 3 inches (8 centimeters) wide.

WHAT RUBBISH!

DANCING QUEEN

Don't try dancing with this way-out creature, unless you fancy a face full of ink! The sea hare flaps its body up and down, and around and around, turning swimming into a hypnotizing rhythmic dance. It produces clouds of reddish-purple ink when disturbed.

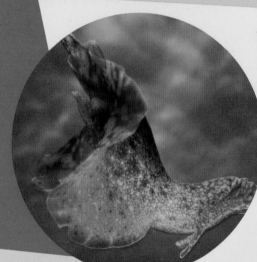

THAT'S ONE UGLY MERMAID!

It's said that dugongs used to be mistaken for mermaids — but it's difficult to see how! Dugongs are far from the graceful sirens of the sea found in the myths. They can grow up to 10 feet (3 meters) in length and weigh over 882 pounds (400 kilograms). Dugongs even have bristles on their upper lips, rather like moustaches!

I LOOK BETTER UPSIDE DOWN!

ANIMALS NAMED AFTER . . .

The
unicorn

Much like the mythical unicorn, the unicornfish has a long horn sticking out of its head. Its horn helps it swim, just like the bow of a ship. Pity it doesn't share the unicorn's magical healing abilities!

The
pineapple

The pineapplefish is yellow and spiny, just like a real pineapple! But don't try to juice one. When they feel threatened, they use spines in their fins to protect themselves. Not-so-smoothie!

The
tulip

Sea tulips may sound like flowers, but forget about putting them in vases! They are a type of sea squirt. They cling to rocks or coral their whole lives and don't move. Many people throughout the world regard them as delicacies.

CHAPTER 5

CAMOUFLAGE & DISGUISE

Now you see them—now you don't! Spectacular skin and fabulous feathers help many critters hide from predators.

The spotted nightjar is hard to spot.

Where's the rocket frog?

SPOT THE ANIMAL

Stumped? It's a tawny frogmouth.

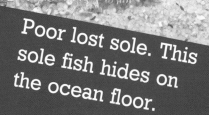

Poor lost sole. This sole fish hides on the ocean floor.

Wood you recognize a fruit-piercing moth?

Leaf-tailed geckos are masters of disguise. They are kitted out with rough skin, a flat body and a leaf-like tail — so they blend in seamlessly on bark, leaves and rocks. These geckos also have clawed feet like a bird, unlike the sticky pads other geckos have. Talk about an identity crisis!

Bright colors don't always mean danger. But you wouldn't want to call this fish's bluff — just in case! The blacksaddle filefish isn't dangerous, even though it looks suspiciously like the crowned toby, which is a poisonous pufferfish. Best not to take any chances!

ONLY BLUFFIN'

BRING IT ON, BRO!

WALKING GARDENS

You've heard of a green thumb, but how about a green claw? Decorator crabs love gardens so much that they plant them on their own bodies! They use their flexible claws to attach sponges to the special Velcro-type bristles on their shells. The sponges continue to grow while on the crab's back.

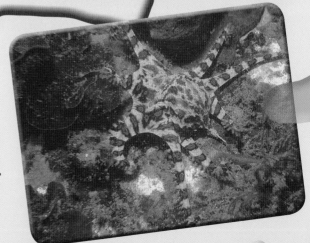

COME BACK WITH MY LAWN!

RING FOR HELP

The blue-ringed octopus is a ruthless killer, but at least it's polite! This poisonous animal has blue rings all over its body, which flash in warning before it attacks. Take the hint and keep away!

ALL THE BETTER TO SEE YOU WITH!

Big eyes mean a big animal, right? Not always! Some octopuses have huge, dark circles surrounding their eyes—not because they had a late night but to make them look bigger than they actually are!

You want a piece of me?

Cuttlefish are great at disguising themselves. Would you believe they even try to look like hippies? Flash a cuttlefish the peace sign with two fingers, and they'll do the same. Sadly, it isn't because they're into flower power! When the cuttlefish feel threatened, they become startled and throw their arms in the air.

SURVIVING EXTREMES

Some animals can survive in the most extreme conditions. From frozen, icy tundras to dry, scorching deserts, many creatures have adapted in crazy and bizarre ways in order to live in these hostile places!

SUPER STRAWS

Ever been thirsty enough to drink a muddy puddle? Be glad you're not a thorny devil! They have to survive in some of the driest conditions on earth. To help them make the most of every drop, thin water channels run between their scales and carry water to their mouths — kind of like the gutters on your roof! Thorny devils can even lie on their stomachs with their legs in the air to absorb water from the ground. Try that next time you're thirsty!

IT'S TIME TO SLIME!

SELF-ABSORBED
FROG

How would you like a coat made of skin and snot? The water-holding frog would love one! It absorbs rain through its skin then stores the water in its tissues and bladder. As soon as the weather dries out, the frog burrows underground. It makes itself a cocoon of mucus and sloughed skin to help it stay nice and moist!

THIRSTY?

Budgies don't need much to drink. In fact, they can survive for about a month without any water at all!

I WISH I WERE A BUDGIE RIGHT NOW...

Some of the most extreme conditions on Earth are found deep under the ocean. Only some truly bizarre creatures can survive the extreme pressures!

UNDER PRESSURE

DEEP SEAL DIVER

Who do you think would win a diving contest — a submarine or a seal? Southern elephant seals can dive for two hours to depths of 1 mile (1.7 kilometers), using just one breath! Humans can only dive to about 591 feet (180 meters), and even reinforced submarines have difficulty reaching the same depth as seals.

Fur seals withstand underwater pressure by collapsing their lungs and dropping their heart rate very low when they dive — sometimes as low as four beats per minute! Thankfully, humans invented scuba tanks so we don't have to do this!

I JUST GOT MY SCUBA LICENCE!

UNDERWATER JETPACK

Are you a fast swimmer? Don't worry if you're not — you could easily come first in a race against the nautilus. Although it can dive up to 1,640 feet (500 meters), it creeps around at a sluggish 6.5 feet (2 meters) per minute. By comparison, humans can swim a 164-foot (50-meter) lap in one minute! The nautilus gets around by using a jet propulsion system in its shell. It may be slow, but the nautilus is resilient — it has survived deep in the ocean for 500 million years and even through the asteroid impact that killed the dinosaurs!

ONE LUNG WONDER

Sea snakes can live their whole lives underwater, even giving birth to live baby snakes at sea. Despite only having one lung, they can stay underwater for up to two hours. They just plug up their nostrils and absorb oxygen through their skin! Sssssspectacular!

When temperatures drop, the environment gets icy and hostile. The extreme creatures that dwell in these cold climates have a tough time keeping warm!

I NOSE IT

Emperor penguins have a clever way to stay warm. They use the warm air they blow out of their nose to warm up the cold air they breathe in. Kind of like a tiny nasal air-conditioner!

HAPPY FEET!

HEY, FANCY PANTS!

Emperor penguins also strut their stuff in fancy feathered pants — a bit like your mom's old legwarmers! Feathered legs are unusual in birds, but this helps to keep the penguins' legs toasty warm in icy conditions.

BRRRRR!

The mountain pygmy possum sleeps under the snow in winter. Its body temperature drops to a chilly 6 °F (2 °C) — that's about the temperature inside your freezer! In fact, this critter is the only marsupial that hibernates under the snow.

FROZEN FROGS

When we think of frogs, we think of swamps, ponds, lily pads and . . . snow? Corroboree frogs can survive in the chilly winters of the Australian Alps. These hardy frogs lay their eggs in ponds that get iced over and covered in snow. When the tadpoles hatch, they are able to swim around in the water underneath the icy surface. Their body temperature may even drop to only a few degrees above freezing. Maybe the tadpoles should be renamed icy poles!

Crocs are big, fearsome creatures. These carnivorous predators are at the top of the food chain and will munch on just about anything ... and anyone! Find out what makes crocodiles, masters of the death roll, so extreme.

TOO HOT TO HANDLE

You know what they say. If you can't handle the heat, get out of the kitchen! Crocodiles may not have many natural threats, but they can't tolerate heat. They like to keep their body temperature at around 86 °F–90 °F (30–32 °C). If they get hotter than 95 °F–97 °F (35–36 °C), they can die!

FAR OUT!

I GOT CAUGHT IN A RIP...

You don't just need to watch out for crocs on riverbanks or by mangroves. Estuarine crocodiles are also known to venture out to sea! They use the currents to swim out to islands and make a tasty snack of little turtle hatchlings. Crunch, crunch!

SOLAR-POWERED CROC

Crocodile skin didn't just evolve so people could turn it into handbags! It traps heat while the crocs are sunbathing, rather like charging solar panels. Infrared cameras have shown that crocodiles have bony ridges on their backs, called scutes, which trap the heat of the sun. They keep the cold-blooded reptile warmer for longer. Just don't try hooking up a lightbulb to one!

CHAPTER 7

TRiPS & TRicks

Mother Nature can be unforgiving. Some animals need to have snazzy tricks up their sleeves just to survive ... even when they don't have any sleeves!

LETTING ONE RIP NOW!

BOTTOMS UP!

Did you know some spiders can make parachutes from their bottoms? They point their bottoms skywards and shoot out a wad of silk, which forms a miniature balloon. The spider then waits for a breeze to catch it and carry them far away. Some spiders have even been spotted as high as 2.5 miles (4 kilometers) in the sky. Look out above you!

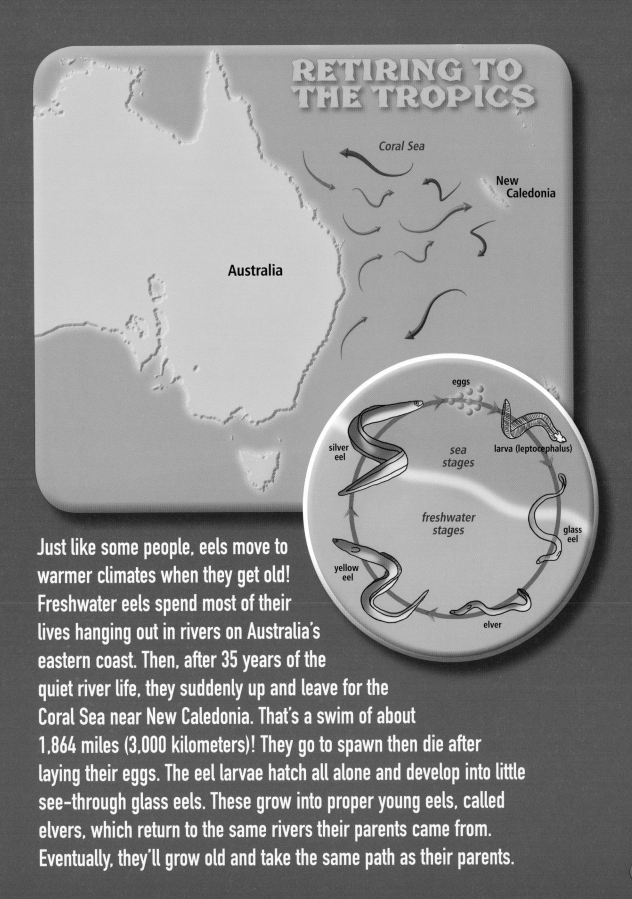

RETIRING TO THE TROPICS

Coral Sea

New Caledonia

Australia

eggs

larva (leptocephalus)

silver eel

sea stages

glass eel

freshwater stages

yellow eel

elver

Just like some people, eels move to warmer climates when they get old! Freshwater eels spend most of their lives hanging out in rivers on Australia's eastern coast. Then, after 35 years of the quiet river life, they suddenly up and leave for the Coral Sea near New Caledonia. That's a swim of about 1,864 miles (3,000 kilometers)! They go to spawn then die after laying their eggs. The eel larvae hatch all alone and develop into little see-through glass eels. These grow into proper young eels, called elvers, which return to the same rivers their parents came from. Eventually, they'll grow old and take the same path as their parents.

GET A GRIP

The osprey has to be careful not to bite off more than it can chew! Its claws grip on so tight that if it picks up a fish that's too heavy, it won't be able to let go. It will be pulled underwater and might drown. It pays to save room for dessert!

STUCK ON YOU

Have you ever wondered why spiders don't get stuck in their own webs? It's because they're smart enough to cover themselves in special slippery oil. They're so slick that they don't stick!

CLOSE THE DOOR, PLEASE!

The trap-door spider makes a special tight-fitting lid for its hole, rather like a bath plug. If predators come knocking, the spider can just hold it shut with its claws. Imagine the fun it could have at Halloween when people come trick-or-treating! Boo!

YOU LEFT THE DOOR OPEN AGAIN!!!

BIG WATER BILLS

Pelicans have massive bills. In fact, the Australian pelican has the longest bill of any bird! Its pouch can hold up to 3.5 gallons (13 liters) of water. That's 13 cartons of milk! Imagine the fish-flavored milkshakes they could make!

SHOP 'TIL YOU DROP

How long does it take your family to do the grocery shopping? Although it might feel like forever, it's probably nowhere near as long as a foraging trip for a female elephant seal. The expedition after the breeding season lasts 75 days! If you think that's bad, the after-the-moult forage lasts for 250 days! Just be grateful it doesn't take that long for your mom to go to the store for your dinner!

WHERE'S THE SEAFOOD AISLE?

KILLER HONEY

Bee honey has special bacteria-killing properties, so it never goes bad. You could even eat honey found in an ancient Egyptian tomb! It wouldn't have spoiled, even after thousands of years. But don't forget to ask your mummy first!

A GHOSTLY SIGHT

According to seafaring legend, it's unlucky to kill an albatross. That's because they're said to be the restless souls of dead sailors. These majestic birds are built for gliding and appear to do it effortlessly while traveling 31-37 miles (50–60 kilometers) per hour.

WHAT A FUN GUY!

Have you ever tried a truffle? They're a type of fungus that grows underground. Truffles are considered a delicacy and are very expensive. Unfortunately for humans who want to get their hands on these tasty morsels, bettongs and potoroos are also fond of these fungi. These pint-sized gourmets are much better at finding them!

WAG IT

How about waggling your bottom for your supper? Willie wagtails are known for waggling their tails from side to side. It probably helps them drive insects out of the grass, which they then snap up. Shake it baby!

45

THAT'S BIZARRE!

GLOSSARY

appetite	a desire or craving for food or drink
bird of prey	a flesh-eating bird, such as an eagle, which has a strong beak and sharp claws
blood vessel	a tube that carries blood around the body
colossal	something very large in size
complex	something complicated and made up of lots of parts connected to each other
constrict	to make something tighter or narrower
crustacean	a type of animal with a hard shell instead of a skeleton that usually lives in water
delicacy	an expensive or tasty food
distract	to take your attention away from what you are doing
expedition	a journey that is undertaken for a special purpose
flexible	something that is easily bent or stretched
forage	to search around for food
formidable	something that causes fear and dread
green thumb	someone who is good at gardening and enjoys it
hibernate	when an animal sleeps in a safe place through the winter
hippie	a person who promotes peace and freedom, especially during the 1960s

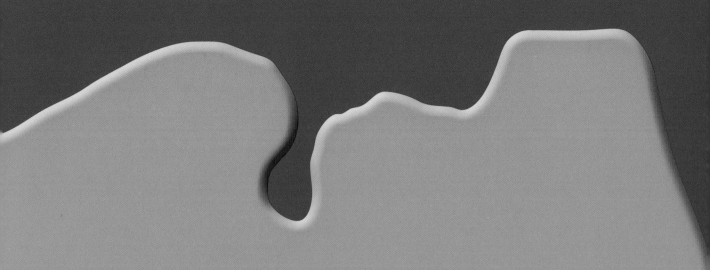

hostile	when something is unfriendly and acts like an enemy
krill	a mass of tiny planktonic crustaceans that some whales eat
larva	the young of any insect that changes the form of its body before it becomes an adult
mound	a pile or a small hill
navigate	to direct or steer on a course to find your way around
nonlethal	something that does not cause death
ripped off	when someone is charged too much money for something
sea anemone	a sea creature that is shaped like a column and has tentacles
sloughed	something that has been shed or cast off, such as a snake's skin
snout	the long nose of an animal
startled	to feel surprised and a little frightened
tofu	a curd made from white soybeans, often used in Asian cooking
tundra	a treeless Arctic plain
venomous	a creature, such as a snake or spider, that can inject its poison into a victim

Additional images:

Mike Gillam/AUSCAPE: p. 21 (marsupial mole); Donald Hobern: p. 28 (fruit-piercing moth) *Eudocima fullonia*/CC BY 2.0, https://www.flickr.com/photos/dhobern/14375017770/; B kimmel: p. 23 (tusked frog) *A Tusked Frog, (Adelotus brevis)*/CC BY-SA 3.0, http://commons.wikimedia.org/wiki/File:Adelotus_tusks.jpg; Ian Morris: pp. 21 (tree-frog eating rodent), 25 (legless lizard) & 39 (estuarine crocodile); Queensland Museum/Jeff Wright: p. 33 (water-holding frog); Ken Stepnell: front cover, pp. 3 & 7 (palm cockatoo); Valerie Taylor: pp. 19 (pearly nautilus) & 30 (southern blue-ringed octopus).

Licences:

http://creativecommons.org/licenses/by/2.0/
http://creativecommons.org/licenses/by-sa/3.0/deed.en